Cathy,
Be blessed
observe God's creation
and what you can learn
about His creation,
Karen Cobb

The Dogs of My Life

And What They Teach Me About the Kingdom of God

KAREN COBBS

authorHOUSE®

AuthorHouse™
1663 Liberty Drive
Bloomington, IN 47403
www.authorhouse.com
Phone: 1 (800) 839-8640

© 2016 Karen Cobbs. All rights reserved.

No part of this book may be reproduced, stored in a retrieval system, or transmitted by any means without the written permission of the author.

Published by AuthorHouse 10/03/2016

ISBN: 978-1-5246-3986-0 (sc)
ISBN: 978-1-5246-3984-6 (hc)
ISBN: 978-1-5246-3985-3 (e)

Library of Congress Control Number: 2016915308

Print information available on the last page.

Any people depicted in stock imagery provided by Thinkstock are models, and such images are being used for illustrative purposes only.
Certain stock imagery © Thinkstock.

This book is printed on acid-free paper.

Because of the dynamic nature of the Internet, any web addresses or links contained in this book may have changed since publication and may no longer be valid. The views expressed in this work are solely those of the author and do not necessarily reflect the views of the publisher, and the publisher hereby disclaims any responsibility for them.

KJV
Scripture quotations marked KJV are from the Holy Bible, King James Version (Authorized Version). First published in 1611. Quoted from the KJV Classic Reference Bible, Copyright © 1983 by The Zondervan Corporation.

CONTENTS

Acknowledgements vii
Introduction ix
Foreword xi
Dedication xiii
A Little Dog Named Biscuit 1
Perfect Or Not, I Love You! 10
Proud To Be With Grand "Paw" 13
Finding Hidden Treasures 14
Biscuit, Don't Worry Be Happy! 16
Joyfully Obedient 18
Brewster 20
For I May Never Pass This Way Again 22
Biscuit Creates A Diversion 23
Good Morning! It's Time To Play 25
Herding The Flock 27
Abby And The Garden Glove 29
Do Not Grow Weary In Doing Good 32
Learning To Walk 34
More Than A Friend 36
Stormy's Encounter With A Skunk 38
The Prodigal Dog 40
Trust And Obey 42
Getting Out Of The Zone 43
Maggie Loves TV 44
Job Well Done 45
Sorrows Will Turn To Joy 47
Why Did He Love Us So Much? 49

No Place To Hide!! 53
Testing The Limits 56
Everyone Needs A Security Blanket 59
I Am With You In The Storm 61
Who Me, A Dog? 65
Walking In His Masters Footsteps 67
Chasing Rabbits 68
Raise Up A Child 69
These Are The Dogs Of My Life 93

ACKNOWLEDGEMENTS

I would like to express my deepest thanks to my friend, Linda, who has encouraged me for years to write this book. She is a God given blessing. "I thank my God in all my remembrance of you," Philippians 1:3.

I would also like to thank my daughter, Molly, who served as editor. Our roles have reversed over the years. When Molly was in elementary, middle, and high school, as well as in college, I edited her papers. Now, she edits mine! Molly has honed her skills as a writer in her work for a government agency where she writes environmental policy and impact assessments and responses to congressional inquiries. She is very good at what she does and her help has been invaluable.

INTRODUCTION

The Dogs of My Life is a collection of stories about just that; the dogs of my life. I grew up with dogs and believe I learned and am still learning many lessons from them. Over the years I have thought about those lessons and what they teach me about the Kingdom of God. Isn't it just like God to use the simplest analogies, (parables), to show us the greatest truths? Each day I marvel at the things my dogs do that either teach me or remind me of something God would have me remember or know.

As you read these stories, I hope you will begin to look at your beloved pets in a whole new way. Look at them as teachers. You will be surprised at you will learn.

Karen Cobbs

FOREWORD

I first met Karen Cobbs at my church. The congregation had just hired her as Music Minister, and I was at my first choir rehearsal with her as director. I was impressed immediately at her command of the music and her skill at directing. What, however, really surprised me was the devotion she gave at the end of the rehearsal. I don't remember what it was about, but I do remember she had taken the most mundane occurrence of her day and made a unique and meaningful spiritual analogy. She continued to do that week after week. Her devotions became the highlight of our rehearsals.

Since that first meeting, we have become close friends, and I am still amazed at the gift she has for finding spiritual lessons in everyday life experiences.

In this book, she combines her love for dogs with her love for God and finds correlations between what she sees in her dogs and what she believes God would have her learn from them.

If you love dogs, you will love this book. If you love God, you will love this book. If you love dogs and God, it is a must for your library.

You will laugh and cry as you read these stories. Hopefully, you too will begin to look for the lessons God would have you learn from the dogs of your life.

Linda Beahm, M.D.

DEDICATION

    I am honored to dedicate this book to my little canine friend, Biscuit. He is one of the dogs of my life though I was not his owner. Biscuit, however, was very special to me. His story, "A LITTLE DOG NAMED BISCUIT" will tug at your heart strings. Biscuit made his family and me laugh and cry. As you read his story, I suspect you will as well. Of all the dogs of my life, I dedicate this book to him because he reminded me of the most important lesson of all.

A LITTLE DOG NAMED BISCUIT

A little dog named Biscuit came into our lives on a warm September day in 2006. I went with my best friend, Linda, to pick a Jack Russell puppy from a litter of 3 month old pups. The dog would be a surprise for her sons.

Dogs and owners pick each other. Though Linda had planned to get a female puppy, this little male kept going back to her, and she kept going back to him. It was meant to be. He was, by far, the largest of the litter and did not look 100% Jack Russell, but he was 100% adorable. He was wire haired with a cute little beard, and all white except for brown spots on his ears. He looked like a biscuit. He stole our hearts immediately.

So began an exciting few years of laughs, immeasurable joy, total companionship, yet, ultimately, heartbreak.

Biscuit had the sweetest, most gentle nature I have ever seen in a dog. That is saying much because all my dogs have been lovable. Biscuit took "gentle and sweet" to a new level. He was the only dog I have ever known who would allow you to take a bone away from him or food from his mouth. He would never growl or snap. He trusted we knew best.

Having always been a dog lover, I loved him as much as I loved my dogs. I delighted at every opportunity to keep him. Often on days when his family was away at school or work, I would go to his house, get him, and bring him home with me. He was such a joy to have around. He was a part of my family. He loved me too. He would turn inside out, with joy, whenever he saw me.

Biscuit had so many mannerisms that would make us smile, laugh, or even cry. He had a sad face we called his power pout. He used this expression when his family was packing for a trip. Often he went with the family on trips, but until he knew for sure if he were going, he would "power pout." It was the most pitiful face you ever saw. His eyes and ears drooped and he would hang his head. We laughed at him, which made him pout all the more. If he did not go with the family, he would come to my house. When he saw me, he was happy again.

Biscuit had a love-hate relationship with birds. He loved barking at them and chasing them, but hated that he could never lift off and soar as they did. But, the game was fun.

Biscuit was fast when he ran, but, more often than not, he did not run; he hopped like a rabbit. He loved hopping with a squeaky ball in his mouth. Each time he hopped, he squeaked!

He also loved the water. Often we would spend long summer days at a lake where his family had a home on a private cove. He was as happy as a clam, swimming effortlessly as his stubbed tail served as a rudder. Back and forth, all day long he would swim trying to catch those pesky dragonflies.

He was a great companion. Linda often worked in her study at home or practiced piano. Wherever she was, Biscuit was at her feet.

The Jack Russell breed is notoriously loyal and protective of the people they love. This trait endeared him more to the family. Linda liked knowing that Biscuit would guard her sons if they were playing in the yard. He was the family protector and a good guard dog who always alerted the family if a stranger came around. Linda would take him with her when she worked late at her office. It was a comfort knowing he would fight to the death to protect her should anyone or anything threaten her. More importantly to Linda, she knew Biscuit would never allow harm to come to her sons.

We enjoy telling a funny story that demonstrates what a fierce protector he was. For several days, Linda and her boys were staying at my home dog sitting for me. Linda's sons were busy doing homework while she was involved in her work. Biscuit was outdoors. They heard him barking ferociously. When she went to investigate, to her surprise, Linda opened the front door to see three police vehicles and a rescue squad vehicle in our driveway. It seems the police dispatcher had received a 911 call from my address. The police had to ping the call to ascertain the location from where the call originated, To this day it remains a mystery how the call came from our house. Neither Linda nor her boys made such call.

Typically, the police would ask Linda if everything was all right. They would likely check her ID and then go into the house to be certain all was well. There was nothing typical about this investigation. Biscuit was holding the offices at bay! They could not get near the house! Linda thought she saw one officer place his hand on his weapon. She told him, in no uncertain terms, he had better not harm her dog. Linda is a very kind and gentle person, but at that point, the officers did not know who held the biggest threat to them; Biscuit or Linda.

The police asked Linda to bring her ID out to them. When they saw that her address did not match my address they became more suspicious. At that point, they wanted to get into the house, but Biscuit would have none of it. They were in a standoff.

After what seemed an eternity, Linda was able to get Biscuit into the house and a bathroom. The officers mustered a little more courage with Biscuit locked away. They came into the house, but Biscuit was about to tear down the bathroom door. Still not wanting to tangle with that little dog, they took a quick peek inside and left. Biscuit had done his job. His family was safe, and the officers went away wondering who had won the standoff; them or Biscuit. Linda, her boys and I had no doubt that Biscuit was the victor. That precious pet had earned his badge that night by holding off three armed police officers.

By all accounts (with the exception of law enforcement) Biscuit was a perfect dog. Over the next couple of years, however, changes began to occur in his disposition. He began to show signs of aggression that went far beyond his protective instincts. Linda and her family would confine him to his yard with the use of a wireless fence. The fence alerted him with a mild electric shock to his collar whenever he crossed the boundary of his yard. Delivery drivers quickly learned not to cross that boundary. They would leave packages at the end of the driveway rather than risk a vicious attack. Once, the neighbor's lawn care man wandered across into Biscuit's yard, and Biscuit attacked. He terrorized passersby.

One day when Biscuit was at my home, our mail carrier came to the door with an item needing a signature. While I tried to hold Biscuit back, he darted past me and lunged at the man, ripping his shirt and taking a big bite out of his stomach. Thankfully, the carrier said he would not report the incident, but the attack was completely unprovoked and raised huge questions about the temperament of this little dog. As sweet as he was, he could and would turn on a dime if he did not know, like or trust you.

Not long after that, a more serious unprovoked attack really got our attention. A mutual friend of Linda's and mine came to my house. Biscuit was outside. This friend got out of her car and started toward the house. Biscuit went into a rage. Before she could react and retreat, he had viciously attacked, leaving a deep bite wound. She shook him off and tried to get back into her car, when, he attacked again. She now had two serious dog bites. There was absolutely no provocation. Our friend would spend the next several hours at the emergency room getting cleaned and stitched. This time, Biscuit was in serious trouble with the law. After a reported dog bite the dog must be quarantined.

After the quarantine, Linda knew she had to address this aggression. One veterinarian recommended euthanasia. There is never a time when a dog's life is above the welfare of a human being, regardless of how much we love the dog. Another option was training. Could we find a trainer who could help Biscuit? We were in luck.

We learned of a trainer who had much experience in dealing with such problems. We had hope. Maybe we could rehabilitate Biscuit.

Biscuits family, my husband and I would attend training sessions for him. In the first session, the trainer had been there less than five minutes when she turned to us and exclaimed, "There is nothing wrong with this dog; it is the people in his life that are crazy!" We were stunned but, she had made a good observation. We were trying to calm Biscuit after his fits of rage, but he perceived our actions as an affirmation of his behavior. There should be no mistake in his mind his actions were wrong; very wrong. This trainer never advocated harsh physical punishment. Spraying him in the face with a mist of water, or dumping a bucket of cold water on him, was enough to get his attention. He had to know he was wrong. Just knowing he had done something to displease the people he loved, obviously hurt him. But still, was it enough?

Every week we took Biscuit to "boot camp." It involved intense obedience classes where he had to interact with other dogs and with people he did not know. The lessons were effective, and he showed much improvement. We all worked very hard to see that Biscuit retained what he had learned. I felt comfortable enough in his rehabilitation that I began bringing him to my house again. Though his behavior was much better, I made him tow the line. Linda was not as sure he was to be trusted. Could we know for certain he had conquered the problem? What if Biscuit attacked a child? As vicious as his previous attacks had been, he could seriously maim or kill a child.

For a couple of years, Biscuit continued to be on good behavior, though he clearly did not like strangers. Most of the time, he was removed from any temptation to misbehave. There were times he seemed to be a perfectly well adjusted little dog. At my house, he was friendlier to delivery people or unexpected guests. I kept a can of rocks nearby at all times. If he got out of line, I would shake the can. That scared him and he would back off. I also kept a spray bottle of water handy. Either of these gentle reminders kept him on good behavior.

Biscuit continued to be the perfect pet for a couple of years. There were, however, alarming signs these aggressive tendencies were beginning to re-surface. Afraid to give him an opportunity for misbehavior, Linda began to board him at a kennel when their family was away, rather than have him stay with me. That made me sad because I missed having him around. However, I did understand, and deep down, agreed.

I did get Biscuit for short periods of time. If Linda's sons had friends over, Biscuit would always come to my house, but usually for a quick overnight stay. On one of those occasions, he charged my neighbor. The man had to run into his home to avoid a nasty attack. As it was summer, these friends were often in their yard. Though very kind, they told me, my two dogs were welcome in their yard, but never again should Biscuit be allowed to run free where he could reach them. No neighbor should be afraid to go into his yard. After that, I knew Biscuit's visits would be few and far between.

In December 2013, Linda asked if I would keep Biscuit overnight. One of her sons had friends over for the night. The weather was cold, and the neighbors weren't likely to be in their yard. I happily agreed though I knew I needed to watch Biscuit carefully. It was a Friday evening when he came. He was such a joy to have around. All was well that night.

The next day started uneventfully. I was expecting someone from Biscuit's family to come for him. About nine-thirty that morning, a neighbor (a different neighbor) came over to use my telephone. Her phone was out of order, and she had to make several calls. Being cautious, I put my little canine friend in a back bedroom and closed the door. He was not happy about being banished and was, loudly, making his displeasure known.

My neighbor was on the phone a long while, so I decided to take Biscuit outside. He happily ran to the back yard, barking at birds and playing with his ball. He had not been out very long when the neighbor finished her calls. Knowing Biscuit was off leash, I walked her to the front door, and went ahead of her to assure she would be safe. Biscuit was still in the back yard. I turned around to help this lady down the steps, when out of nowhere Biscuit appeared and lunged at the unsuspecting, elderly neighbor.

I was horrified. So was she. Thankfully, my neighbor was wearing a thick coat. Rather than taking a chunk out of the lady, Biscuit ripped the garment instead. I screamed at Biscuit and tried to grab him, but he was gone as quickly as he came. He knew he had done a bad thing. Once again, his attack was absolutely without provocation. Biscuit had a serious problem.

I prayed that morning someone would come for him. I should have taken him home, but I did not.

Later that morning I went out to play with Biscuit and my two dogs. I kept Biscuit close to me. I did not believe there would be another incident that day. I did not want to take any chances.

We had not been out long when a car pulled into my driveway. I did not recognize the vehicle or the driver. It was not unusual for an unfamiliar car to stop. My dogs are incredible Frisbee players, and often people stop to watch them play or ask questions about how to train a dog to do what they do. I am always happy and proud to take the time to talk with anyone about my dogs. This latest visitor was indeed, there to admire my canine athletes and their skill at playing Frisbee. In the blink of an eye, Biscuit darted toward her vehicle. It never occurred to the visitor, a dog lover, that he would attack her. I was frantic. I began screaming, "Get back into the car! Get back into the car!" She could not understand I was trying to warn her. She took one step and Biscuit attacked. Drawing away from him, he missed her. She quickly stepped back into the car, but Biscuit pursued her. Before she could close the door, he had jumped into the car far enough to get his teeth into her leg. As she pulled the door closed, Biscuit loosened his grip and backed away. She was now safe inside the car, but, too late to avoid damage. Twice in one day he had gone into an unprovoked rage. He was completely out of control.

The victim did not believe Biscuit had broken the skin. She had on blue jeans, and denim is sturdy. She assured me she was okay, but also said she had never seen a dog attack the way he did. Again, though not threatened in any way, he behaved as if he were fighting for his life.

It was a long afternoon, and it wasn't until early evening Linda came to get Biscuit. I had her come in and sit down while I broke the news to her regarding the events of the day. No one could mistake the pain in her eyes. Biscuit now had three strikes against him. He would eventually hurt someone; maybe badly.

The next afternoon there was a knock on my door. Upon opening the door, there stood the visitor from the day before. I invited her in. Before she would enter, she wanted to know if Biscuit were there. Upon learning he was not, she said she had to talk with me. We sat, and she explained upon arriving back at her home the prior day, she looked at the bite and found it had broken the skin. Naturally, she wanted to be to certain he was current on vaccinations. Having taken him myself for those treatments, I assured her he was. She was agonizing over what her next move should be. She knew if she reported the incident, officials would have to euthanize him as he now had three strikes against him. She could not bear the thought of breaking the family's heart, especially so close to Christmas. She remained, however, torn over the possibility Biscuit could cause serious injury or death to a child. There was no easy answer. Sadly, I assured her I was certain the decision was already made. I had not talked with Linda since the prior day, but knowing her as I do, I knew she had made the hard choice.

Later that day I went to see her. We sat and talked; Biscuit at our feet. I told her of the visit from earlier in the day. We were both crying. I was right. She had made the decision. This precious little animal was too dangerous to have around unsuspecting strangers.

We talked and cried a long while. Was there any other way? Not really. Even if Linda gave Biscuit to another family, he was no less a threat, and she could not live with the thought he might be endangering someone. She never wavered. Agonizing as it was, it was the right decision. We only talked about when to do it. Could it wait until after the holidays? No, it could not. He was like a ticking time bomb; a bomb we had to disarm.

Linda is a busy person, and I knew she had not the time, nor the energy, to deal with this over the next couple of weeks. I offered to take him whenever she could arrange with the veterinarian to do it.

The veterinarian was a friend and confirmed to her that she was making the right decision. Many times he had counseled dog owners in a similar dilemma to euthanize the pet. Often those he counseled delayed and lived to regret not heeding his advice. He also warned that Biscuit's aggression would likely get worse with age.

In Virginia, there is a waiting period of ten days after a bite before the euthanasia could take place. The veterinarian agreed to do it. The date would be December 17.

Biscuit was allowed to spend those days at home under house arrest. Linda took great care that he had no contact with anyone except the family. It was a difficult ten days. We shed many tears. Biscuit, however, enjoyed the time. He was allowed to sneak onto his favorite furniture, get extra treats and sleep on the bed; all of which were never allowed before. Even a person on death row gets some perks before the execution.

The thought of this as an execution bothered Linda the most. She was sending this little dog to his death, yet he was the perfect family pet. It did not seem fair. Life and death are not always fair.

On December 17, Linda's sons and husband said their goodbyes to Biscuit. She, Biscuit and I left for the veterinarian's office. Linda drove, and I held Biscuit, feeding him treats all the way. It was the end of the work day, and the doctor was waiting for us.

Linda signed some papers while I held my little buddy. Other patrons with their pets in the waiting area talked about how cute he was. One even spoke to him and said she hoped Santa Claus would be good to him. It broke my heart.

We took him into a back room where Biscuit would receive the lethal injection. The doctor was very kind and allowed us a few minutes to say goodbye. Then, he placed Biscuit on a table and put the needle in his veins. Biscuit died, licking Linda's hand. It was peaceful and quick. Even as I write about it, I can't hold back the tears. He will always be one of the most special little dogs I have ever known.

This story is long and detailed. It is much more so than any other story in this collection. In everyday life events, I like to find a spiritual analogy. What does God want to teach me, show me, or remind me of in these daily occurrences? As I thought about Biscuit, it became apparent.

Biscuit was his own worst enemy, and he was powerless to save himself from himself. Though he had that very good nature, there was also a dark side. In animals, we call it their primal nature. In people, we call it our carnal nature or sinful nature.

Just as Biscuit could not save himself from his primal nature, we cannot save ourselves from our sinful nature. God knew we would forever be slaves to the sinful nature and therefore, separated from Him. But God also had the answer. "For God, so loved, the world that He gave His only Son, that whosoever believes in Him, shall not perish but have everlasting life." John 3:16. Jesus, the Son, would be the answer for all humanity for all generations. On the cross, Jesus took on the sins of the world. The Bible tells us, "He who knew no sin, became sin for us so that we might become the righteousness of God in Him." 2 Corinthians 5:21. By accepting His sacrifice, our sins will forever be nailed to the cross of Jesus.

The story does not end on the cross. The resurrection of Jesus, the ascension into heaven, and the sending of the Holy Spirit are all a part of this great story. It begins, however, with Jesus taking the blame for our sins so that we might live.

Wow, that is so awesome! We don't have to be perfect, though we should always try. We will always have a sinful nature. We only need to let the Perfect One, Jesus, pay our debt and then, we must live our lives in gratitude for His sacrifice.

The analogy isn't perfect because there is a different standard of accountability for animals. There would be no redemption of sin for Biscuit. He suffered death because of it.

Biscuit did not have a Savior. Praise God, we do!

PERFECT OR NOT, I LOVE YOU!

Having only one child, I always wondered how a parent could love each of his or her children the same. I always thought I could never love a second child as much as my one and only. My dogs taught me you could love each equally and they showed me a much more important truth.

I have two border collies. They could not possibly be more different.

Stormy is the perfect dog!! He is beautiful, fiercely loyal, fun, intelligent, gentle, obedient, and a great companion. He does no wrong. He hates to get dirty. He avoids mud puddles but, if he should get dirty, he carefully cleans himself before coming inside. Stormy spends his days trying to be everything you want him to be. His purpose in life is to please his master. With him, it is all about what he can do for you. There is nothing about Stormy that is not perfect.

Then, there is Maggie! Maggie is also beautiful, sweet, fun and intelligent. However, Maggie has a mind of her own. She is far from perfect. As a matter of fact, I call her my "train wreck." She is a high maintenance dog. She has much energy and needs constant attention. She is curious and precocious and can look at a mud puddle and get dirty. With Maggie, it is all about her, never about what she can do to be that perfect dog you had hoped she would be.

One would think I must love Stormy, my perfect dog, more than Maggie, my train wreck. That is not the case. I love them both equally. I can't imagine choosing one over the other. As I pondered this, I began to realize how God, Who has a perfect Son, Jesus, loves me with all my imperfections, just as much.

The Bible says, "He who knew no sin, became sin for us so that we might have the righteousness of God in Him," 2 Corinthians 5:21.

Unfortunately, Maggie cannot become the perfect dog just by being with Stormy. We, however, can achieve the "righteousness of God", by spending time with Jesus. In our mortal bodies, we will never be perfect, but in accepting Jesus as the perfect blood sacrifice and obediently following Him, God will count it as righteousness.

Perfect or not, He loves us all the same.

PROUD TO BE WITH GRAND "PAW"

Yes, that's right; Grand Paw, not Grandpa. From the day we got Stormy we referred to my husband, Joe, as Stormy's Grand "Paw". There was nothing Stormy liked better than to be with Grand Paw.

One of the rituals that Joe established with Stormy, very early in their relationship, always made me laugh, and it never got old. Stormy would wait outside when it was time for Joe to come home. Joe would pull just a few feet into the driveway, and Stormy would run to meet him. Joe would open the door to his truck, and Stormy would jump into the vehicle to ride the rest of the way, all fifty feet of it, with his Grand Paw. The trip only took a few seconds, but Stormy loved it. He would sit with his head held high, and a great big beautiful smile on his face. (Yes, dog's smile.) How proud and happy he was for every second he could spend with His master.

Christians should be so happy and proud to spend every second possible with the Master. Do you realize what an honor it is to have the God of the universe, invite us to spend every minute of our lives with Him? God would love to see us with our heads held high and smiles on our faces when in His presence. Sadly, most of us, do not proudly accept His gracious invitation often enough.

Today, would you proudly spend time with the Master? Talk with Him and walk with Him. The bonus is, it is not just the "50 feet to the end of the driveway", but anywhere, everywhere, all day, every day.

FINDING HIDDEN TREASURES

I am sure all pet owners have special rituals with their pets. The ritual might be something before mealtime, before a walk, or at play time. Whatever the ritual, it is fun for us to observe these incredible creatures that God has given us and delight in the companionship we share with them.

Years ago I started one such ritual with our border collie, Stormy, and it continued when we added Maggie to the pack. Each night while the dogs were out for the last time, I would take tiny treats and hide them all over the house. When they came back in, the race was on to see which one could find the most, the fastest. Stormy was especially good at this. We called him the "vacuum" as he, seemingly, sucked in the treats as he passed by them. They would get so excited at this nightly game. After they had found all the goodies, they would eagerly await one large dog biscuit, at which time the game was over. It did not take them long to discover all the hiding places and the game was not as challenging, but they loved it just the same. They never tired of it, and I never tired of watching their delight as they scooped up all the hidden treasures.

Though Stormy is no longer with us, I still do this ritual every night with Maggie. She enjoys not having competition.

Our Heavenly Father has hidden treasures for us everywhere. Maybe at first, we have to look harder for them, just as Stormy and Maggie had to look harder at first. It may be the beauty of a sunrise or sunset, the sound of children's laughter, the majestic power of a thunderstorm, a rainbow reminding of God's promises, or watching waves roll into shore from the ocean. As we discover and enjoy each treasure, we must be aware of a larger treasure; the still small voice of God that speaks to us in all our daily finds. He reminds us in each of these treasures that He loves us, is ever with us, and nothing can pluck us from His hand. The treasures are there. We just need to find and enjoy them.

BISCUIT, DON'T WORRY BE HAPPY!

Over the years I have known my friend Linda, we have often loaded my dogs, Stormy and Maggie, and her dog Biscuit, into the car and with her family we would head to Smith Mountain Lake, VA. This man-made lake, developed to power a hydroelectric plant, has grown into one of the state's favorite vacation and recreational areas. Many beautiful homes line the shores of the lake. Linda's parents lived at Smith Mountain Lake, and we enjoyed many visits, especially in the summertime.

Their home was on a private cove, so it was safe for dogs and children to be on the water, away from the many boats that navigated the main channels. Biscuit cared nothing about those things. He only knew it was a special place where he could run and play with his buddies, get extra treats from Linda's mother, and swim in the lake, chasing pesky dragonflies all day.

We made our 45-minute journey so often the dogs began to recognize the route. To Biscuit's dismay, it was the same highway that passed by his veterinarian's office. Biscuit loved going to the lake but did not like going to the doctor. While my dogs were excited to be on that road, Biscuit never knew if he should worry or be happy. Until we passed his doctor's office, he would worry. When Biscuit worried, he had an unusual whine. He would yawn while whining. It was funny, but an annoying sound. We called it his power whine. He would be distraught until he saw us drive past the doctor's office. After that, the whining would stop because he knew we were going to the lake where he could "run and play, with his buddies get extra treats from Linda's mother, and swim in the lake chasing pesky dragonflies, all day." What a difference in his demeanor when the worrying stopped. He had gone through all that worry for nothing.

The truth is, Biscuit never needed to fret at all. Why didn't he know wherever we took him, we would care for him? Didn't he know worrying would not add one minute to his life?

That story has a compelling analogy to apply to our lives.

Jesus said, "Look at the birds of the air; they do not sow or reap or store away in barns, and yet your heavenly Father feeds them. Are you not much more valuable than they? Can any one of you, by worrying add a single hour to your life?" Matthew 6: 26-27.

Worry is a sure sign we don't know or believe our Heavenly Father is in control. Biscuit had no way of controlling where we might take him, and he also did not trust we would do what was best for him.

Often we have no control over the circumstances in which we find ourselves. At those times we must know Who does have control. When we start trusting our instincts instead of trusting God, we have reason to worry. Often we are in situations where we may exercise some control over the outcome. Seeking God and His wisdom in making the right decisions will allow us to proceed without worry.

Therefore, rest in the knowledge that God loves us, and is in control of every aspect of our lives. Don't worry, be happy!

JOYFULLY OBEDIENT

Maggie is always eager to play in the mornings. Stormy never was as anxious to play. He was content to watch Maggie. However, I always felt I needed to engage him in some activity while Maggie was having so much fun.

One morning, while walking out to get the newspaper, it occurred to me delivering the paper to the door would be a good job for Stormy. It was at the end of the driveway, rolled and secured with a rubber band. It would be easy for him to pick up and bring to me. Stormy was eager to learn and anxious to please. It took all of five minutes for me to teach him to go out, grab the paper and deliver it to my door.

This daily chore became Stormy's favorite thing to do. At first, he would forget unless I asked, but as soon as I said, "Stormy, get my paper," he was off like a bolt of lightning. After several days, I did not have to ask. It was the first thing he did when he went out. When he had the paper in his mouth, he would trot proudly back to me, his tail wagging, and a smile on his face and he would drop it at my feet. I don't think anything he ever did warmed my heart more than to see the joy he had in obeying this simple command. He loved it so much that when I stopped getting the newspaper, I continued to take a rolled paper out to the edge of the driveway for him to bring to me. Several times a day, I would sneak out and place a paper there so he could retrieve it over and over again.

I was reminded this week of Stormy and how much he loved delivering the newspaper. I began to wonder if I serve my Master with as much joy. I wondered how many times I, reluctantly, agreed to serve my Master in some capacity. How many times have I said "no," when a position needed filling at church, or, "yes, I'll do it but only if you can't find anyone else!" The truth is, many of us begrudgingly give time to serve the Master. Often, we would rather be somewhere else on Sunday morning than in Sunday School and worship. We would rather watch television than spend time with Him or serve Him.

Stormy never hesitated. Whenever I gave him a command, he could not obey fast enough. Oh, that we could be so joyfully obedient!

I am not suggesting we jump into every job needing to be done for the Kingdom. Often, trying to do too much leads to burnout. The Bible is clear. God has given every church body the resources it needs to function properly. If it is a position God has gifted you to do and you are passionate about, likely He is calling you to do it. You should pray about it and go where the answer leads.

I doubt Stormy prayed, but he took great pleasure in being obedient to his call. Once again Stormy showed me a valuable lesson. When the Master calls, obey. You'll be happy you did.

BREWSTER

It was mid-December, 1999. Brewster, my basset hound, had been in failing health and I knew he would not be with us much longer.

At the time, we lived in a split foyer home. This design has lower and upper levels. Brewster's condition prevented him from climbing stairs, so he entered on the lower level and stayed there. I entered and went upstairs. I liked having him nearby, but he spent most of his last days alone.

On that mid-December day, I walked downstairs to our family room. My plan was to sit beside Brewster and wrap Christmas presents. As I entered the family room, I spoke to Brewster. I walked across the room to light the gas logs. While I was there, Brewster made a strange sound. It was not a bark, nor was it a cough. It sounded more like a gasp. At that moment I thought nothing of it, other than it was a different sound than I had ever heard him make. I had already decorated and with Christmas music playing and fire logs lit, the afternoon promised to be delightful. I finished with the gas logs and walked back to Brewster. When I sat down beside him, he did not move. I stroked his coat and began to talk to him. There was no response. Brewster was dead! The gasp I heard was his last breath.

I was devastated. I thought how I had not a chance to say "goodbye." It was a Sunday, and I had been away at church all morning. He had been alone all day. I wondered if he died thinking I did not love him. Had I known he was dying I would have stayed with him. Now, it was too late. I would never have the chance to tell him how special he was to me. The expectation of a pleasant afternoon turned to sorrow.

I have thought of that day many times over the years. It still grieves me. I have lived with regrets since that time.

Often it's hard to spend time with those we love. Our busy lives prevent us from seeing them. The point, however, is clear. None of us knows when we may lose a family member, friend, or a beloved pet. We should take every opportunity to express our love and say the things we need to say.

Life is short. Let there be no regrets.

FOR I MAY NEVER PASS THIS WAY AGAIN

I have always found it amusing that male dogs "mark" their territory wherever they go. Every tree, every mailbox, every utility pole, every fire hydrant, and seemingly, every blade of grass must be "marked".

One day, as I was walking my little dachshund, Percy, I marveled at how he always seemed to have a drop left no matter how many times we had stopped for him to mark a spot. It is a way of stating,"I have been here before, and this territory is mine!" Another dog then comes along and tries to claim the spot, and on, and on, and on it goes.

That day I was reminded of a lovely song I had heard many, years before. I thought about the song, "I May Never Pass This Way Again," as Percy and I finished our walk. While I don't remember all the words, the gist of it is we all leave a mark, good or bad, wherever we go and whatever we do. We should, therefore, make every effort to leave something positive behind.

The last words of the song,"I'll give my hand, I'll sing my song, I'll share my faith because I may never pass this way again" are a challenge. It says to me I must always look for ways to give my hand, sing my song and share my faith in a way that changes the world for the better. Some people I will never see again. I have to get it right the first time.

That day Percy reminded me at the end of the day, I want to be proud of what I have left behind. Maybe only a word of encouragement, a helping hand, or a statement of faith, will be all someone needs to make a difference in his or her life. I can do that! I must do that for I may never pass that way again.

Thanks, Percy for showing me in a most unusual way this valuable lesson.

BISCUIT CREATES A DIVERSION

I was dog-sitting my friend's dog, Biscuit, while she was away. I had Percy and Stormy at the time and three dogs can be a handful when they are not playing well together. That day, I gave each a rawhide chew bone. You would think it would make each one happy, but each always seemed to want the bone one of the others had. That particular day, Biscuit had lost his bone. He was annoyed that Stormy and Percy were happily crunching away on their bones. Biscuit whined, and worried, and tried his best to steal a bone from one of the other dogs. They would have none of it.

I have always been amazed at how smart our border collies are, but Biscuit took a backseat to no dog when it came to intellect. While having no luck getting a bone away from either Stormy or Percy, Biscuit suddenly ran to the front door, barking as though he had heard a visitor. When he did this, Stormy and Percy dropped their bones and also ran to the door, howling. Much to their surprise, there was no one at the door, but Biscuit had diverted their attention long enough to run back into the room and snatch up a chew bone, leaving Stormy and Percy wondering what had happened.

I have laughed at that incident so many times, and I believe it has a great spiritual takeaway. Consider this: Satan constantly tries to divert our attention from things that God would have us do. Like Biscuit, Satan is on the sideline whining that we are about Kingdom work. Unlike Biscuit, Satan is not at all interested in what we are doing; he only wants to keep us from doing it. That's when he creates the diversions. Suddenly we can find any number of reasons to stop working for the Kingdom and start operating in more worldly endeavors.

For example, Satan made it very attractive to consumers to do their shopping on Sundays. Now the blue laws are meaningless. Many who should take Sunday as a day of rest now must work on Sundays for their livelihood. Many churches are "encouraged" to finish the Sunday morning service early so the congregants can get to their favorite restaurants before the Sunday crowd hits. Little League Baseball teams now play their games on Sunday mornings. Now that is a diversion! Given a choice, would most children like to play ball or go to church? As a society, we have allowed secular humanism to creep into every aspect of our lives. As Christians, we should be ashamed this has happened before our eyes and often sanctioned by our churches and us.

Satan is diverting our attention from the prize. He does not want it; he just does not want us to have it. He is here to steal, and kill and destroy, (John 10:10) and the whole time we are falling for his tricks, he is taking our prize. In Philippians 3:14 the Apostle Paul says, "I press on toward the goal to win the prize for which God has called me heavenward in Christ Jesus."

I am not sure which dog, Stormy or Percy, lost his chew bone to Biscuit that day, but my dogs allowed the diversion. We should never allow Satan to distract us from pressing on toward the goal and winning the prize. As Christians, we must remain on high alert. Our enemy is always trying to turn our attention to matters that are temporal rather than eternal. He just wants to steal our chew bone!

GOOD MORNING! IT'S TIME TO PLAY.

I have been a night person all my life. The night is my most productive time. The hardest thing I do each day is getting out of bed in the morning. That is not the case with my dog, Maggie. She awakes eager to start her day of work catching Frisbees and chasing golf balls or tennis balls. She has boundless energy in the morning. When I can barely open my eyes, she is shoving a Frisbee in my face. Reluctantly, I dress and drag myself outdoors, often in the rain or snow, to play Frisbee or ball.

I think how nice it would be to start my day with such joy and expectation. I am never awake enough to do my daily devotions in the morning. At the very least, I should do what Maggie appears to do in her canine kind of way. In her mind, she must be thinking, "This is a new day to play. I will rejoice and be glad in it." Sound a little familiar? She puts me to shame, because I know the first thought that crosses my mind when I awake should be, "This is the day that the Lord has made. I will rejoice and be glad in it," Psalm 118.24. I should say, "Good morning Lord. What great things do you have planned for me today to advance Your Kingdom on earth?" Regretfully, most mornings that is not what I am thinking. I just want to go back to sleep.

However, as I write this, I accept the challenge from my little bundle of morning energy. I will resolve to approach the day with as much joy and expectation as does she.

I am not sure why I am a night person. A day has 24 hours. I do believe God would have me use my waking hours to seek and serve Him. Whether we are day people or night people, we should rejoice in every moment to serve the God of the universe.

Thank you, Maggie, for reminding me that every day belongs to the Master. I will rejoice and be glad in each day, even if I only have one eye open!

HERDING THE FLOCK

Maggie is a high energy, focused and intelligent border collie. Most border collies are known for these traits, as well as their instinctive herding abilities.

The breed can be content all day long herding sheep, cattle, horses, or whatever herd or flock is available. Unfortunately, we live in town and don't have herds of animals. Maggie has to herd anything and everything else. She runs the boundaries of our property containing anything already on the property and fiercely protecting it from intruders. Border collies need to work and without a job for her, we have to be creative in providing her the stimulation she needs to be happy and healthy.

Without a herd, Maggie obsesses with play. Her favorite activity is catching Frisbee. In a sense, her Frisbees are her herd. While she never tires, I do.

Because we live in town, we have a leash law. Our dogs cannot leave our property unless on a leash. We have a wireless electric fence that gently reminds Maggie she needs to stay on her property. Maggie is terrified of the mild electric shock she gets when she crosses the boundary. The correction is not harsh, but effective.

Often when playing with her, a Frisbee will land over the borderline. When this happens, Maggie will go as far as she can to retrieve it. While she does not cross the line, she will lie down, never taking her eyes off the wayward Frisbee. None of the other Frisbees are as important to her when one is "out of the flock." I eventually have to retrieve it because I can't wait as long as she can.

Once, when this happened, I was reminded of the parable of the Good Shepherd, Matthew 18: 12-14. In the parable, Jesus talks about the good Shepherd, who, when one out of a hundred sheep goes astray, will leave the ninety-nine to find and bring back to safety the lost one. It is not that He does not love the ninety-nine, but he knows they are safe. The Good Shepherd wants all His sheep safe in the fold.

That's what God wants for us. However, he allows us freedom to wander away. The Good Shepherd, Jesus, is always calling us back to the fold.

Just as the ninety-nine sheep had safety in numbers, Christians need a network of other Christians to provide support in the difficult times of their lives. When we are tempted to wander, other Christians gently lead us back to the fold and make us accountable.

Maggie protects her little herd of Frisbees. Our Good Shepherd protects His flock and gives us safety in numbers.

ABBY AND THE GARDEN GLOVE

Though this collection of dog stories is about the dogs of my life, sometimes I share one of these stories with friends. Recently, a friend commented that she had a story about her dog, Abby. I instantly saw a spiritual analogy.

One day, Abby's "mom," Karen, was working in her garden. When she finished, she took off her gardening gloves and put them down with her tools. A short while later, Karen went to get the gloves only to find one was missing. She looked around but found it nowhere. Karen immediately suspected Abby had something to do with its disappearance. Abby liked chewing on all sorts of things, and a gardening glove would greatly appeal to her.

As Karen looked for the glove, she saw Abby with a piece of it hanging from her mouth. As Karen rushed to retrieve the glove, Abby saw her coming and quickly took one final gulp. The glove was gone!

Karen and her husband Ricky were frantic. The glove was not something that would digest properly. It could get lodged in her digestive tract and cause a life-threatening blockage. Ricky rushed Abby to the doctor where, after a period of retching and vomiting, the glove came up. That certainly was not a very pleasant experience for Abby. I suspect the glove coming back up was not nearly as satisfying as going down.

It reminds me of how we are often attracted by things that turn out to be bad for us. We spend our lives chasing rainbows; always looking for the thrill, or the next best thing, only to find the joy we thought it would bring, only brought disappointment or sorrow.

The Bible tells us in Proverbs, "Delight yourself in the Lord, and He will give you the desires of your heart," Psalm 37:4. How often is that verse misunderstood? I know it does not mean if we delight ourselves in Him,

He will give us everything we want. Instead, I think it means He changes our priorities. He will provide us the things that will last for eternity, not things that are here today and gone tomorrow.

Abby has owners that love her very much. She could never want for a better life. Still, however, Abby longs for that one thing that will give her temporary pleasure. If she only knew, she has everything she will ever need. So do we. If we seek Him, He will give us more than we could ever hope for, for all eternity.

DO NOT GROW WEARY IN DOING GOOD

My stories about Maggie often have some reference to her love of play. No matter what the activity, she is always ready. Whenever we take her near a baseball, football, or soccer field, she is likely to disrupt a game by running onto the field and grabbing the ball!

One of her favorite pastimes is retrieving golf balls. I love to play golf, and I always keep a bucket of balls handy so she can retrieve them when I practice chipping and pitching.

This week we were out on an unusually hot day. She was running hard, chasing balls and bringing them back to me. As her coat is mostly black, it absorbs the intense heat of the sun. I could tell it was beginning to get to her. I kept hitting the balls, but eventually she was too weary to play. I looked around and there she was, resting in the shade of the apple tree. I laughed at her, and the first thing that came to my mind to say was, "Maggie, do not grow weary in doing good." I immediately thought of the scripture Galatians 6:9. The Apostle Paul entreats the church at Galatia to "not grow weary in doing good, for at the proper time we will reap a harvest if we do not give up."

I am sure each of us has been involved in a project, whether at church, work, community, or some philanthropic endeavor, and we are tired and ready to give up because we don't see any fruit of our labor. This verse is heartening because God, through the Apostle Paul, is telling us we will see results if we keep going; if we do not grow weary. If we are persistent even when we are uncomfortable, or exhausted, we will reap rewards.

I don't think Maggie should continue retrieving balls until she drops dead of a heat stroke, but I do believe God used her that day to remind me of something I already know. God does reward our tireless efforts on His behalf. We should never grow weary in doing good!

LEARNING TO WALK

Our little Dachshund, Percy, was a precocious little guy who enjoyed running, playing, and chasing his ball. One day we noticed he seemed to be in pain when trying to walk. We watched carefully, but several days later his condition had worsened. He could not walk. There was paralysis in his hind legs

His breed is predisposed to spinal problems and injuries. I took him to his veterinarian, and she immediately scheduled him for surgery at the Virginia Tech School of Veterinary Medicine. It was a two and a half hour drive to Blacksburg, Virginia. A team of doctors was waiting to do surgery. If it were successful, he would possibly walk again; if not, he would remain paralyzed.

The doctors did the surgery immediately, and then came the long wait to see if he would recover. We took him home a week after surgery. At that time he was still paralyzed, but the doctors said the surgery went well, and he would need healing time for us to be sure. Several weeks went by and we anxiously watched and waited for improvement.

Percy was somewhat mobile because he could pull himself forward with the use of his strong front legs. One morning my husband and I were following Percy as he dragged himself down the hallway in our house. Suddenly, Percy pushed up with his back legs and took a step! We were ecstatic. It was like watching your child take his or her first step. We could not contain our joy as we jumped up and down, laughing and crying at the same time. It was only one step, but we knew he had regained feeling and mobility in those hind legs. In just a few days, he was up walking and running as though nothing had ever happened.

That was more than twenty years ago but I remember it as though it were yesterday. It always reminds me our Heavenly Father loves to see us take our first baby steps as Christians. From the time each of us accepts Jesus as Lord and Savior, the attempt to walk begins. Some take in all the nourishment that God offers through prayer, Bible study, and fellowship with other Christians. They quickly have the strength to take that first step, then another, until they are up and running and helping others to get up and running. I have this picture in my mind of a loving God looking down upon us and laughing with joy as we take those first steps. I can picture the same loving God, saddened that we never seem to get out of spiritual infancy. He loves us no less, but He wants us to enjoy the abundant life that comes from growing as Christians and discovering the keys to the Kingdom.

We would have been sad had Percy not recovered, but we would have loved him still. That little dog brought us much joy for many years after that surgery. In his way, Percy must have been grateful to have a second chance.

Our God is a God of second chances. We can learn to walk anytime we choose.

MORE THAN A FRIEND

We are so blessed to live in a neighborhood with wonderful people. One of our neighbors is Bryan. Bryan and his wife Joyce, and their children Kyler and Kirsten are a lovely family and have become good friends. Not only have they befriended my husband and me but our dogs as well.

Bryan is a dog lover and fell in love with Stormy and Maggie very soon after moving into the neighborhood. He was the caretaker for his sick, elderly mother. Whenever he had a chance, he would come over to our house to play with my dogs. They loved it, and it gave Bryan a badly needed break.

Stormy especially looked forward to his visits and often waited in our yard, gazing longingly toward Bryan's house until he came out. Stormy would just about turn inside out when he saw him coming. Bryan always got down on the grass and wrestled with him. Stormy loved the play time and adored Bryan. It was a mutual friendship. Those visits with Stormy were therapeutic in the purest sense and helped Bryan cope during difficult times with his mother. The bond Stormy and Bryan formed was heartwarming.

That relationship is an example of the millions of such relationships that man has with a dog. If you have never had this connection with a dog, you might wonder if I, and the millions of others, am a little crazy. Maybe I am. I believe, however, God uses these unique relationships to teach us how we are to minister to others.

That fact became apparent to me when I saw the weariness and anxiety leave Bryan's face as he played with Stormy. Thinking about Bryan's and Stormy's relationship, I realize I don't often bring joy to friends, family, neighbors and even strangers as naturally as did Stormy.

If God gives us our special pets to bring joy, companionship, and friendship, how much more does he expect of us? The question is rhetorical, but the answer is clear. He places us here to do the everyday work of ministry. What we get in return will likely be far more than we give. God used Stormy to be a blessing to Bryan.

Is God using you and me to be a blessing to those around us? Spend time today looking for ways to bless someone. It could be your presence will help lift a burden or lessen despair in someone's life. That should come as natural to us as it did Stormy. Once again, Stormy puts me to shame.

STORMY'S ENCOUNTER WITH A SKUNK

Stormy never did anything intentionally to displease us because he was our "perfect" dog. However, occasionally he would happen upon a situation that was beyond his control

On two occasions, Stormy happened upon those cute little nocturnal animals that would defend themselves by expressing a defense mechanism which had a horrible smell. You guessed it. Stormy had encountered a skunk.

I remember well, the first time this happened. It was a rainy, summer night. There was no lightning nor thunder, just a steady rain. I knew, immediately when I opened the door to call Stormy in, he had gotten the worst end, literally, of the encounter with the skunk.

The next couple of hours would be challenging. I could not allow Stormy to come into the house, and I did not have anything outside, except a garden hose, to wash the stench away. It was midnight, and my best friend had stopped by for a visit before leaving the next day on a business trip. Being the friend she is, she stayed and helped.

We had both heard the best way to neutralize the odor, is to bath in tomato juice. I had none, and at midnight, in a small town, there are few places open. Fortunately, Walmart was, and my friend drove across town and bought, what must have been, every can of tomato juice in the store.

Then began the hard work of getting Stormy clean. In the pouring rain, with a garden hose, we bathed Stormy in tomato juice and then rinsed. We bathed and rinsed again. We did this for quite a while and finally began to smell some improvement. The worst of the odor was on his face, which took the direct hit. Bathing around his eyes was difficult. It took several months for the smell on his face to disappear.

When the clean up was over, we were all drenched and exhausted. I don't know how I would have managed on my own. Thank God for precious friends who will do anything in the time of need.

As I think back on this, I realize Stormy had no idea what would happen when he approached that strange animal. After all, this little creature looked like a cat, and aren't dogs supposed to chase cats? It was the most normal thing in the world to do.

I felt sorry for him because the spray from the skunk must have burned his eyes badly. It did mine just being close to Stormy.

Stormy's curiosity caused my friend and me a lot of trouble that night, and it caused Stormy some as well. Remember, Stormy was my "perfect dog." He would have never wandered into that mess had he known it would cause him or me any problems.

Therein is the spiritual analogy. We try so hard as Christians, to do the right thing. We never want or intend to displease God, and we certainly don't want to bring problems on ourselves. However, we are products of a fallen world, and we are born with a nature that causes us to, sometimes, do bad things.

The Apostle Paul put it this way: "I do not understand what I do. For what I want to do, I do not do, but what I hate, I do," Romans 7:15. What a challenge it is for Christians to do the right thing. We always want to, but often we don't. We have no control, just has Stormy had no control.

That is why we need God's grace. Grace means unmerited favor. Though we do not deserve it, He offers us salvation through the shed blood of Jesus. That blood washes us clean.

About a year later, Stormy had another encounter with a skunk. He did not want to do that; he just could not help himself. We still offered him our unconditional love and washed him clean again.

That is what God's grace does for us. With His unconditional love, He makes us whole again, even when we don't deserve it.

THE PRODIGAL DOG

I had Biscuit at my home for the day. I often kept him for my friend Linda when she and her family were at work and school. I loved having Biscuit at my house. He was a delightful little dog.

Biscuit loved being outside, so I let him out to play. After a while, I went to check on him. He was not in my yard. I called, and he did not come. He had run away.

I was frantic. All sorts of things started running through my mind. Biscuit was not street smart. I was afraid of a car hitting him. What if someone picked him up and I would never see him again. What would my friend say? I worried most about her little boys who adored Biscuit. Would they ever forgive me for losing him?

I walked up and down our street calling. I eventually got in my car and drove through the entire neighborhood. I knocked on doors asking people if they had seen a cute little white dog roaming around; no Biscuit.

Just when I believed there was nothing left to do the thought came to me to go to his home. Biscuit's family lived a half mile from me. He was still a puppy, and I did not believe he would find his home. I drove there just the same. As I pulled into his driveway, much to my surprise and delight, there on the carport, was Biscuit, waiting by the door for someone to let him in. I was so happy to see him. I did not scold him for running away. I suspect being lost was punishment enough.

Do you remember the parable of the Prodigal Son? Biscuit's runaway reminds me of that story. In the Bible's account, the son of a wealthy landowner decides to take his inheritance and leave and seek riches elsewhere. While away, he squandered his riches and when a famine came to the land he had no money or food. He worked as a servant just to get food the pigs ate. The Bible says he "came to his senses," and realized he could have plenty of good food as a servant in his father's home. He decided to go back. In the story, the father saw him coming from afar and ran to meet him, had compassion on him, embraced him, and kissed him. Rather than scold the son, the father threw a party. Overjoyed the father exclaimed, "My son who was lost is found!" Luke 15:24.

I know how overjoyed I was that Biscuit decided to go home. Imagine a parent whose child has run away. Imagine how thrilled the parent would be to have that child come back? Now, imagine how a loving God is overjoyed when one of His own comes back to him.

If I had found Biscuit wandering the neighborhood, I would have forced him to go back with me. Instead, he decided nowhere could be better than home where he was loved and protected from a dangerous world.

When we wander away from God, He doesn't force us to come back to Him. I believe He has a gentle way of persuasion, but the decision is ours to go back. How overjoyed He must be when we realize there is no better place to be than in His care.

TRUST AND OBEY

My husband and I live in Bedford, VA, a quiet, sleepy town in the foothills of the Blue Ridge Mountains. We moved here from a city about twenty miles away. While we were building our new home in Bedford, we rented a house. It was on a busy street. I had to watch the dogs carefully.

One day I was sitting on the porch and Stormy was nearby in the yard. A squirrel darted across the yard past Stormy and into the street. When Stormy saw the squirrel, he took off in hot pursuit. From my vantage point, I could see an oncoming vehicle on a collision course with Stormy. Cars parked on the street blocked the view from the approaching driver. Knowing this could end very badly, I screamed, "Stormy, come!" It was as though Stormy had brakes. He stopped immediately, turned around and came to me. I was thankful he was safe. He was so because he was obedient.

We had owned Stormy for several years and he had come to love us completely. Through that love he came to trust us. We had spent years developing that relationship with him. That love and trust likely saved his life that day.

The analogy is clear. Jesus told his followers: "If you love me, you will keep my commands," John 14:15 NIV. It is that simple. If we have not developed an intimate relationship with the Lord Jesus, we will often not obey Him because we won't trust Him. We won't know Him. We are only safe in the arms of Jesus if we abide in Him. Trust and obey. There is no other way.

GETTING OUT OF THE ZONE

Whenever we are out and about town, we usually take the dogs. It gives them a chance to go for a ride, and we hate leaving them home alone.

It is amusing to watch them observe the world around them. Of course, the dogs notice everything, especially cats and other dogs. Border collies seem to want a certain order in their lives. They don't like change, and they don't like things out of place. Lots of things are out of place around town!

On our walks through the neighborhood at Christmas, they are frightened at displays in the yards. Maggie especially gets spooked at the huge inflated Santa in one neighbor's yard. She gets nervous if I move a piece of furniture. Once, when I moved a picture from one wall to another, she barked until I moved it back!

As I think about their paranoia, I realize they are not unlike people. We often resist change and retreat from situations that may be different from our usual routines. Perhaps there is nothing wrong with that. However, I believe God wants us to get out of our comfort zones and explore what opportunities He may have for us beyond that zone. They are all around us; a lonely person who may want to talk, a homebound neighbor that may need groceries, children that need mentors, shut-ins who may enjoy getting a card in the mail, or people in jail or prison who would benefit from a visit. The opportunities are endless.

Today, resolve to venture out of your comfort zone and do something to make the world a better place.

MAGGIE LOVES TV

My husband and I are amused at how our border collie, Maggie, becomes engaged when we are watching television. She sits directly in front of the set and reacts to what she sees and especially loves the dog commercials or any shows that feature dogs or animated characters. I marveled at her one night when her favorite commercial was airing. Maggie was in another room but came running when she heard the jingle playing. One night she was particularly excited while watching a basketball game. I did not understand it at first, but after a while, I had realized she wanted the ball!

Maggie is not a couch potato. She would rather spend her waking hours doing more productive activities, such as chasing balls and Frisbees.

Most of us should learn from Maggie. We should devote more time to worthwhile endeavors and less time in front of the box.

I enjoy watching TV and it can be a source of family fun provided the selection of shows is wholesome. Maggie loves it but would much rather spend time with her master. Wow! That's an idea. What if we were to take the time we spend in front of the set and instead spend that time with the Master! Wouldn't our relationship with Him grow stronger?

Resolve today to find more time to fellowship with the Lord, Jesus. It may mean giving up some television time, or some other pastime. God wants us to enjoy our leisurely activities, but not at the expense of a relationship with Him.

JOB WELL DONE

We said "goodbye" to our beloved dog Stormy yesterday. The pain of losing him is unbearable.

Stormy became very sick a few weeks ago. A trip to his doctor and some blood work indicated he had hepatitis. The doctor did not know the cause, but given what had been overall good health, she believed it to be viral in nature. With other dogs, she had been successful in treating the condition. I started him immediately on a vigorous treatment plan. She and I were confident he would make a full recovery.

After ten days, without seeing improvement, I called the doctor. She knew if he had not recovered after ten days of the treatment regimen, he would not recover. It was apparent the cause of the hepatitis was not viral in nature. He had late stage liver cancer.

I was devastated, but I had already known in my heart his condition was more serious than we had originally thought. In the prior week, he refused to eat yet his body began retaining massive amounts of fluid which filled his abdominal and thoracic cavities and spread into his limbs. Fluid had surrounded his heart. His breathing became labored. Stormy was dying.

One of the most painful realizations for me that day was discovering he did not have days to live; he had hours. He made it through that night, and I took him to the veterinary hospital the next morning. The doctor did tests and x-rays to confirm the diagnosis from the afternoon before. It was Friday, and it was evident he would not live through the weekend. Had I tried to take him home to die, he would have suffered. The doctor recommended euthanasia that day.

My husband, Joe, was not with me, and I knew he would want to see Stormy, and I felt we should make the hard decision together. I took him home with a plan to take Stormy back to the hospital later that afternoon.

Joe was no more ready to hear the diagnosis than I. Neither of us could believe we would have to let Stormy go that day. We talked about it a long while. Joe had doubts. He had not seen the x-rays or spoken to the doctor. Rather than push Joe to a decision, we agreed to take Stormy back to the hospital where Joe could see the evidence first hand. Once he did, the call was easy. We would say goodbye to Stormy within the hour.

The staff and doctor were very kind. They allowed us some time with Stormy. Stormy lay comfortably on a quilt while Joe and I petted him and cried. We were not ready to let him go, but we knew the decision was the right one for Stormy.

When the doctor came back into the room to give Stormy the injection that that would humanely take his life, there were many things I wanted to say to the most special dog I had ever known. Naturally, I wanted to tell him how much I loved him, and how precious he was to the family and me. But, instead of saying those things, the first words from my mouth, were, "job well done!"

In the eleven years we had him, he was the perfect pet, companion, and friend. He was a selfless dog who only wanted to make those around him happy.

I often took him to a nursing home to visit the residents. He never had the training to be a therapy dog; he just was, instinctively. Everyone adored him, and he adored them in return. It was heartwarming to see the smiles he brought to so many faces and to see his big, happy smile in return. (Yes, dogs smile.)

As I think about him and how well he had done his job, I think how I want my Master, at the end of my life, to say, "Job well done, my good and faithful servant." Matthew 25:21. Isn't that why we are placed on this earth? We are to serve Him and others selflessly and to bring joy and happiness wherever we can.

Stormy made the world a better place. He existed to serve his master.

Stormy taught me many life lessons; lessons that my Master wants me to learn. Today the question is, do I serve my Master as selflessly as Stormy served me? I hope so. At the end of my life, I want to hear those words, "job well done."

SORROWS WILL TURN TO JOY

It has been several months since I said goodbye to our beloved border collie, Stormy. I think of him often and the pain of losing him is unbearable still. Having had him so long, I find myself looking for him, momentarily forgetting he is gone. One such lapse in memory happened recently.

It was a beautiful spring day. After a long, cold winter, I was ready to play golf. I loaded my clubs into the trunk of my car, but left the trunk open. I left the golf bag leaning out of the trunk so I could easily reach and grab a club to practice pitching and chipping in our yard. Maggie loved retrieving balls and the practice time was not only good for me but her as well.

Now, let me backtrack just a few months to the previous Christmas. My daughter had given me a border collie headcover for my driver. Even the most serious golfers have funny headcovers. Looking at it reminded me of Stormy. The cover was clearly in view as I walked out to the yard.

When I finished my practice, I headed back to the car and saw the border collie headcover. At that moment I had one of those mental lapses when I thought Stormy was still with me. I began to chuckle at how cute it was that Stormy had jumped into the trunk of my car so as to be sure he went with me to the golf course. If just for a split second, he was with me again. Quickly I came to my senses and realized it was only a headcover and not Stormy in the trunk. Just that quickly, my joy turned to sorrow.

As I thought about this, I have been reminded the Bible tells us, in heaven there will be the exact opposite; our sorrow will turn to joy. What a glorious thought!

I don't know if I will see Stormy in heaven, though I have heard great arguments that we will see and know our pets there. I only know I will have joy.

Isn't it a comfort to have confidence all of our troubles, hardships, and sorrows are but a moment in the grand scheme of eternity with God.

That said, I am still sad when I reach for that driver and see that headcover. One day, my sadness will be no more.

WHY DID HE LOVE US SO MUCH?

Perhaps you have already read the story of our perfect dog, Stormy. We loved him so much because he was the once in a lifetime dog. He existed only to please us and, that, he did.

Today, as I was thinking about Stormy and how much we loved him, the question came to me, "We know why we loved him, but why did he love us so much?."

The story goes back about eleven years. Stormy was born and spent the first two years of his life in the quiet little town of Salmon, Idaho. Our daughter, Molly, lived there with her border collie, Scout. Often she, and other dog owners would walk their dogs through the lovely, tree-lined neighborhoods. On their walks, they would pass a house where a beautiful border collie was tied in the yard. The precious dog always enjoyed seeing someone and having a kind word spoken to him. He apparently responded to kindness, but from the way he looked and the condition of his surroundings, it was equally evident he had not experienced much kindness in his two years. At best he was terribly neglected, and, at worst, abused.

Stormy became the "project" of the dog lovers who walked that route. The townspeople would take him toys, and treats and just spend a few moments giving this lovely creature a little of the love he deserved. The next day, the toys would be gone and Stormy just as alone. He loved the times that people stopped.

There was an elementary school playground behind Stormy's yard. One teacher remarked that it broke her heart to see him longingly wanting to play with the children, but, always, just out of reach. Stormy became this teacher's mission. The mission was to rescue him and find a home where he would be cared for and loved.

The Dogs of My Life

At Christmas time our daughter came back to Virginia to celebrate Christmas with us. The school teacher, also on Christmas break, had been working behind the scenes to complete her mission. She went to Stormy's home, talked with his owners, and bought him from them. I think she would have and possibly did, pay a dear price for him. No one would ever know for sure what she had to pay to rescue this very special dog.

After the holidays, our daughter returned to Idaho and to work. Her first morning back, she walked into her office, and there, tied to her desk chair with a note, was Stormy! The message said the dog was being given to her because it was evident that Molly loved dogs, and the anonymous donor knew she would give Stormy the home he deserved. We have a joke in our family that border collies are like potato chips; you can't have just one! Now she had two.

Molly took Stormy to her home, where he, for the first time, had a home. For a long while, Molly did not know the kind lady that rescued him. She would eventually find out through a mutual friend of hers and the teacher.

Now, the story continues. If Stormy belonged to Molly, how did my husband and I come to have him?

A couple of months after Molly got Stormy, she moved from Salmon, Idaho to Ft. Collins, Colorado. After being in Ft Collins only a couple of days, she sustained a serious sports injury which required her to be in a cast and on crutches for several months. Molly called and explained in her condition it was hard to handle one dog, and most certainly not two. She wanted to know if we would take Stormy for a few months until she healed. I had no hesitation about having another dog, but, I remember saying to her, "Molly, you know how I fall in love with dogs. What happens if I fall in love with him?" She answered, "If you fall in love with him, he is yours." She does not remember telling me that, but, needless to say, she never got him back!

My husband and I drove to Ft. Collins the next day. Molly had gotten us a hotel room since she was sharing an apartment with two other young ladies, and there was no room for us to stay with her. When we arrived at the hotel, Molly was standing outside with Stormy. It was love at first sight! I had never seen a more beautiful animal. We could tell he loved us immediately too. Stormy and my husband formed a bond right away. They would be best buddies for the next eleven years.

Molly knew how much we loved Stormy and how much he loved us, so there was never a question about when or if she would get him back. We are grateful to her for such a wonderful gift.

We took Stormy home. He was part of the family until he died a few months ago. He could not have had a more perfect, happy life. He never would long for love and affection again. He was, indeed, rescued.

I have gone into great detail to explain to you Stormy's early years, his rescue, and how we came to have him. You should be able to understand why he loved us. We, along with the teacher and Molly, had rescued him from a life with no joy and no hope.

The analogy is clear. I pondered the question, "Why does Stormy love us so much?" It became apparent to me this is why we should love Jesus so much. Stormy had no hope. It only took someone who loved him enough to rescue him from a life of hopelessness, despair, and misery, for him to become all he was created to be! Our enemy, Satan, only comes to steal, kill and destroy, John 10:10. Jesus, on the other hand, stands at the door and knocks. If we open that door, our hearts, to Him and invite Him in, he will rescue us from a life of hopelessness and despair.

It is tragic that we live in a fallen world and innocent animals, like Stormy, are victims of this fallen state, as are we. Satan even uses poor, defenseless animals to play his dirty tricks.

Once we brought Stormy into our family, he could not do enough to show us how much he loved us and how proud he was to be our dog. He was no longer destined to live a life of hopeless despair.

As Christians, neither are we. Do we show our Master how proud we are to be in His family and how happy we are he chose to rescue us? Our condition without Him is every bit as hopeless as was Stormy's. Take time today to show Jesus how much you love him. In gratitude, thank Him for rescuing you.

NO PLACE TO HIDE!!

Maggie had an appointment today with our veterinarian. As I took her in, I realized it was the first time she had ever been to the doctor without Stormy also going. Stormy died several months ago. I had always taken both of them, even if only one had to see the doctor. They gave each other much needed moral support.

I used to be so amused at how they would each try to hide under the chairs in the examining room, so as not to be found by the doctor! The staff at the veterinary hospital is kind and caring, but my dogs hated being there. Stormy usually beat Maggie to the hiding place. Once, when she thought she had nowhere to hide, Maggie went to a corner in the room, sat back on her haunches and put her face in the corner. I suppose she thought if she couldn't see the doctor, then surely the doctor could not see her. I still laugh when I think about that little dog in the corner, trying to hide.

The truth is, it is a tiny examination room and, try as they might, neither could escape. The doctor would come in, find them immediately, and do what she had to do even if it were not pleasant for them. She only acted in the dog's best interest.

It reminded me that none of us could hide from God. The Bible says He has numbered every hair on our heads. If He knows us that intimately, surely there is nothing we can ever hide from Him. He is gentle, kind, and loving. He could never act, except in our best interest, even if it were not pleasant for us. We may spend a good portion of our lives trying to run and hide. He knows, however, where we are, and eventually, we have to come to the point of reckoning.

While I find it funny my dogs think they can hide, it is far from funny when we believe we can hide from God.

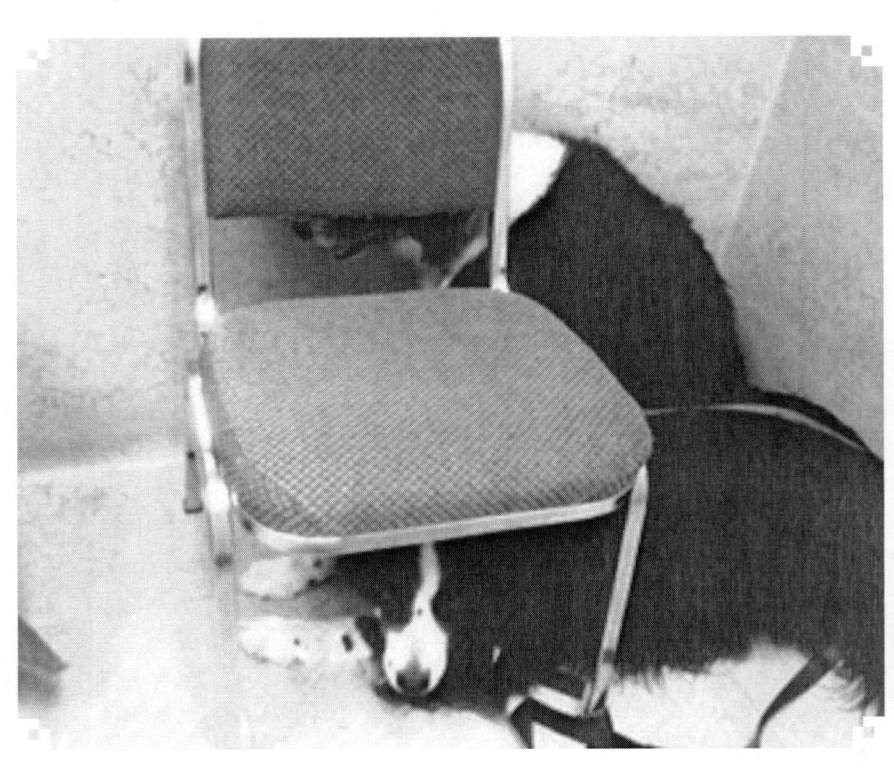

Today, don't hide from Him. Embrace His presence, ask Him to forgive any known sin, and be thankful our Heavenly Father loves us so much and allows us to fellowship with Him, all day, every day. We break that fellowship when we are trying to hide from Him.

TESTING THE LIMITS

We live on a street that has a fair amount of traffic. Naturally, this causes some anxiety unless we have a means of keeping our dogs from going to the street where there would be potential for injury or even death.

Our yard does not have a traditional fence, but we do have a wireless fence. The components of the wireless device include a transmitter that transmits a signal to a receiver that is attached to the dog's collar. The transmitter allows us to set a radius perimeter that the dogs stay within. Should they approach the boundary, the transmitter transmits a harmless beeping signal to the collar to warn the dogs that they are getting too close to the limit. Should the dogs keep going, the transmitter sends a mild electric shock to the collar. This shock frightens them, and they run back into the yard. The shock is harmless, but it works. More often than not, we do not use the collars. For several reasons, it is easier to remove them. Once the dogs learn the boundaries, they don't need the collars. The problem is, the longer they go without the collars, the more they test their limits. After a couple of weeks without a shock, they will venture further and further. If they go too far, they may be on the street which is far more perilous to them.

I want my dogs safe, and I watch very carefully to see they are not testing the limits. When they do, the collars go back on, and they hear the beep or feel the shock when they go too far. It only takes hearing the beep or feeling the shock once, to bring them back to the reality that pushing the limits has consequences.

Pushing the limits may be hazardous for my dogs. Pushing the limits can be dangerous for humans, as well. God has established certain parameters for us and when we push those parameters we get in trouble. It may not be deadly, but we run the risk of losing fellowship with God.

God gives these limits to keep us safely in the fold. He wants us to abide in His presence where He protects us from the danger of worldly influences. Does this mean no harm will ever come to us? No! None of us will escape the perils of this world altogether. In a fallen world, bad things will happen to good people. However, when we trust our lives to His care and follow His rules, we clothe ourselves with His protective cover. Then, we know whatever befalls us, we are abiding in His divine will and nothing can separate us from Him.

My dogs get into enough trouble even when they stay within their defined boundaries. They don't need to make it worse by breaking the rules. Likewise, we don't need to complicate our lives by testing the rules God has laid out for us.

EVERYONE NEEDS A SECURITY BLANKET

We got Maggie when she was a puppy. From the first night we brought her home, she would cuddle up with a fleece blanket, gather it in her little paws, stuff it in her mouth and suck on it until she fell asleep. Even after she was asleep, she would still be sucking it. She was so much like a baby.

It reminded me of my daughter who, as a child, found security in that one, special blanket. I remember it was hard to get it away from her long enough to launder. She still has it to this day.

The funny thing about Maggie is even though she is now a full grown eight-year-old, adult dog; she still lies down with her blanket, gathers it in her front paws, stuffs it in her mouth and sucks on it until she goes sleep.

As I think about this practice, I realize we all have a longing for security. We all want to feel safe and at peace. The Bible tells us, "No weapon formed against us, shall prosper," Isaiah 54:17 NIV. Isn't that real security? Knowing the God of the universe has "blanketed" us with His protection gives us an inner security and peace that passes understanding.

The Bible is rich with verses that remind us of His protection and care. Here are just a few. "Whenever I am afraid I will trust in You, (God)," Psalm 56:3 NIV. "Even though I walk through the valley of the shadow of death, I will fear no evil, for You are with me, Your rod and Your staff, they comfort me," Psalm 23:4. "You will keep in perfect peace, him whose mind is steadfast, because he trusts in You," Isaiah 26:3 NIV. "Do not be anxious about anything, but in prayer and petition, with thanksgiving, present your requests to God, and the peace of God, which transcends all understanding, will guard your hearts and your minds in Christ Jesus," Philippians 6-7 NIV.

Such verses as these can be found throughout the Bible. Commit them to memory and when the storms of your life are pressing in and stealing your peace, recite them over and over again. We don't need a security blanket; we need the blanket of God's security.

God's blanket of protection is the best security we can have. Bad things will happen to us, and we will be afraid, but when we trust He is in control, ours fears will subside and we will enjoy perfect peace.

I AM WITH YOU IN THE STORM

Our Maggie is an Alpha dog. She likes to control other dogs. Though she is very sweet and gentle with people, she likes to be the top dog. However, if another dog were to challenge her dominance, she would back down, tuck her tail and run. While she puts on this act of toughness, she is a wimp!

Like many dogs, she is frightened of thunderstorms. At the first sound of thunder, she tries to find a quiet, safe place. In a severe storm there is never a quiet place, nor, to her, a safe place.

When we know a big storm is coming, we like to hold Maggie to calm her. Several nights ago one such storm was brewing. We knew she was inside, but could not find her anywhere. We checked all the usual hiding places with no luck. The storm was getting worse, and Maggie was lost somewhere inside our house, and we did not have a clue where else to look.

We had walked through the house several times. Apparently on one walk through, we had closed the pantry door which had been ajar. What we did not know was Maggie had gone into the pantry and crawled to the back, behind a scrub bucket. Her collar had become hooked on the handle of the bucket, so when she moved, the bucket moved, which scared her all the more. While checking once again in the kitchen, my husband Joe heard some commotion in the pantry, opened the door and found her, huddling and trembling behind the bucket!!

It is sad to see how traumatized she becomes when I know she is safe with me, and I will keep her from harm. I want to say "Maggie, don't you know that neither thunder, nor lightning, nor wind, nor rain, nor hail, nor things that go boom in the night, nor anything else can ever separate you from my love?"

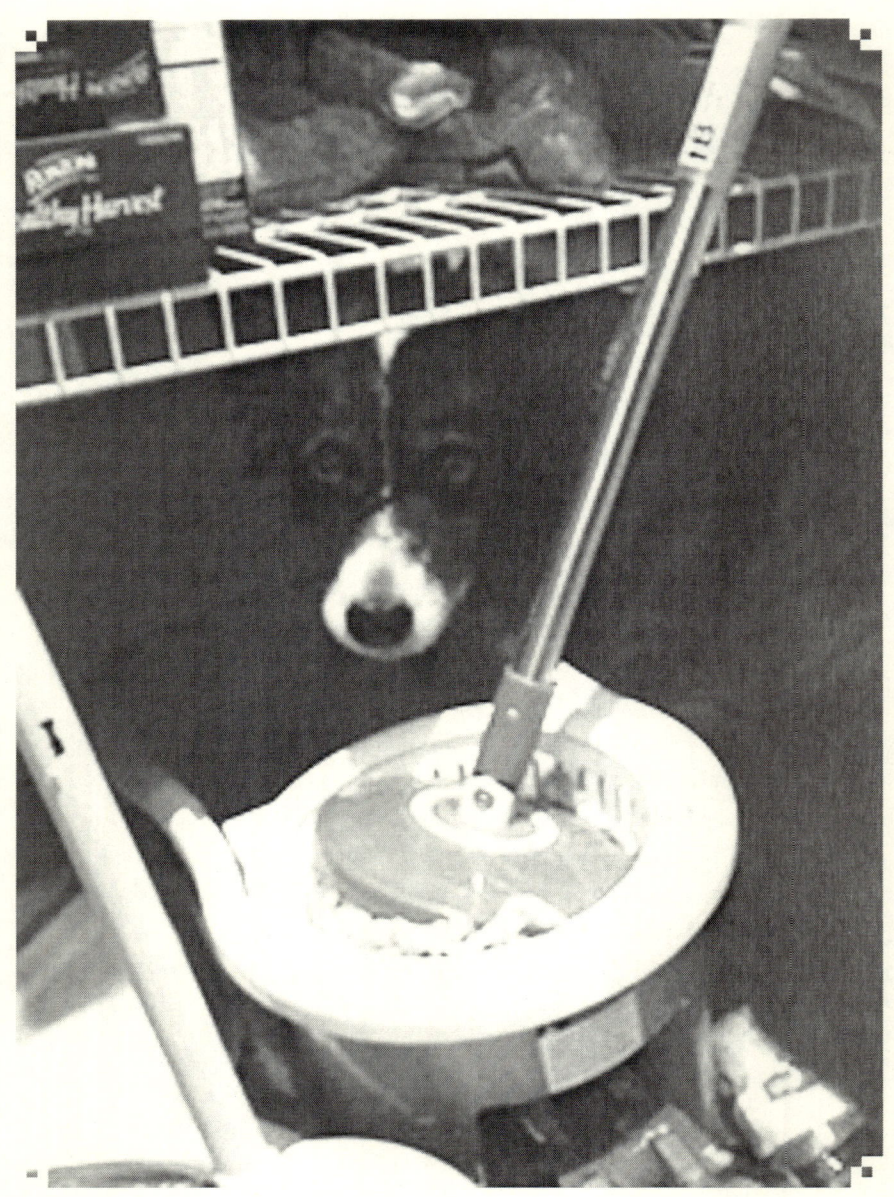

Sound familiar? Yes! Remember the Apostle Paul speaking to the church at Rome? "For I am convinced that neither death nor life, neither angels nor demons, neither the present nor the future, nor any powers, neither height nor depth, nor anything else in all creation, will be able to separate us from the love of God that is in Christ Jesus our Lord." Romans 8:38-39 NIV. That passage is one of my favorites, and I try to remember it when I am facing a trial of some kind.

Just as I want Maggie to know that I would do everything in my power to keep her safe, our God is assuring us that nothing that happens can separate us from Him and His love.

Maggie is eight years old at this writing, and she has never learned that my husband and I will protect her in the storm. Even sadder is the fact, often Christians never learn God is faithful to His word and He is with us no matter what is going on in our lives. There is no problem, no concern, no worry, no condition, no situation that will ever separate us from the love of God.

Today, bask in the irrefutable truth that His love is always with us, no matter how bad the storm.

WHO ME, A DOG?

One thing all dearly beloved dogs seem to have in common is that none believes he or she is "really" a dog! After all, we have made these incredible creatures members of the family. How often have you heard a dog owner say something like, "Oh, my dog does not know he is a dog; he thinks he is a person." If you are reading this and you have a dog, in my mind's eye, I can see you nodding your head!

Though I have found this common in all the dogs of my life, my friend's little dog Twinkle truly does not have a clue she is a dog. As a matter of fact, she not only thinks she is a person but, more than that, a Princess; above ordinary humans. It is hilarious to be around her and watch her use her charm. She knows how to get what she wants and everyone is at her beck and call. She is cute, and she knows how to use that to her advantage.

While I think Twinkle is precious with her haughty attitude, it reminds me that human beings should be the exact opposite. If anyone ever had a reason to be haughty, it was Jesus. After all, He was the only begotten Son of God. The Bible tells us in Philippians 2: 5-11, NIV, "Your attitude should be the same as that of Christ Jesus; who being in very nature, God, did not consider equality with God, something to be grasped, but made himself nothing, taking the very nature of a servant, being made in human likeness, being found in appearance as a man, he humbled himself and became obedient to death, even death on a cross! Therefore, God exalted him to the highest place and gave him a name above every name, that at the name of Jesus, every knee should bow in heaven and earth, and every tongue confess that Jesus Christ is Lord, to the glory of God the Father."

Wow!! That is so powerful. Jesus, who is equal to God, did not assume that role, but, rather, in obedience took on the attitude of a servant. In humbling himself, God, therefore, exalted him.

That's what God wants from us; a servant attitude, humility, and obedience. We don't do this to be exalted. Neither did Jesus. Jesus did these things, as should we, to advance the Kingdom of God on earth. Our reward will be in heaven.

Somehow, I don't think Twinkle will ever understand that, and, she shouldn't. She is doing what God created her to do; making her family happy. She does bring to mind, though, this great lesson on servanthood, obedience, and humility.

WALKING IN HIS MASTERS FOOTSTEPS

One of the things so special about Stormy was how completely trusting and loyal he was, especially to my husband, Joe. Joe was Stormy's master. Wherever Joe was, Stormy was there also. We often thought of him as Joe's shadow. If Joe was watching TV, Stormy was lying by his side. If Joe walked 25 feet to the kitchen, Stormy was one step behind, in Joe's footsteps. I thought it was interesting that Stormy never presumed to be equal to his master but was happy to follow closely behind. Stormy completely trusted his master would not lead him into harm's way.

On the other hand, whenever it was clear that Joe was going to take Stormy for a walk, Stormy would happily walk by Joe's side as if to the enjoy fellowship. And enjoy it he did! Nothing made Stormy happier than to be with his master.

The analogy is clear. Oh, that we could be so trusting of our Master that we would follow Him anywhere, never questioning, just trusting. At times we may just want to be by His side enjoying fellowship with Him.

The Master loves us unconditionally and always has our best interests at heart. Maybe, at times we presume to know more about our well being than the Master does. We often want to be equal or even superior when it comes to navigating life's rocky roads. If we would only follow in His steps, we would never go astray, and would avoid the inevitable pitfalls we encounter when we try to do it on our own.

Stormy knew to leave it to his master to lead the way. The challenge for each of us today is to let our Master show us the way and to follow in His footsteps. If walking by His side in times of fellowship, learn to talk to Him and to listen to Him. Get accustomed to asking Jesus in every question of our lives to show the way and then, follow His lead.

CHASING RABBITS

I went out to play with Maggie this morning. She is always excited about playing, but especially so in the mornings.

It was a warm spring morning and she was in good form chasing one Frisbee after another. Suddenly, she dropped her Frisbee and darted behind the shrubbery in front of our house. She was frantically chasing something, in and about the flowers and shrubs. As I was not sure I wanted to know what it was, I stood back and let the drama unfold. As Maggie ran behind one bush, out from the front of another came an adorable baby rabbit. It quickly scurried across our driveway to the other side of the house while Maggie was still trying to find the object of her chase.

Later, as I pondered this, it reminded me how most of us spend our lives "chasing rabbits." We are always after that elusive dream. We want the next best thing; the biggest car, house, boat or smartphone. Sometimes we even achieve the dream only to find, maybe, it was not what we wanted at all.

God would have us stop chasing rabbits and start seeking first His Kingdom. "Seek Ye first the Kingdom of God and all these things will be added unto you," (Matthew 6:33). That does not mean when we seek Him first He will give us everything we want. It means if He is the object of our chase, we can receive all He has ever wanted to give us and more than we will ever need.

He is trying to give us the keys to the Kingdom, and we're chasing rabbits!

RAISE UP A CHILD

When our daughter was a baby, my husband and I loved to awaken to her cooing in the nursery. After a couple of months, the cooing turned to babbling but still nonsensical. Like all parents, we waited for the day she would say something we could understand. Would it be dada or mama?

We had two dogs at the time; Happy and Shadrach. Molly was fascinated with these creatures.

One morning we awoke, as usual, to her babbling. Happy loved her and went to the nursery whenever he heard her. She obviously was pleased her little buddy had come in. She enjoyed reaching through the rungs of her crib to pet him. That morning, from across the hall, she said it; her first word; HAPPY! It was the most natural thing in the world for her to say. He was her friend. She had known him since she was born and she loved him and trusted him.

In our bedroom, we heard it and laughed. Neither of us would have bragging rights on which name she spoke first, but we were nonetheless thrilled our baby girl had started to talk. (She has never stopped!)

I have told that story many times over the years, but today as I was thinking back on that morning, it occurred to me that Molly has never known a home without dogs. In her few short months, she had learned to love them and treat them as her best friends. She never had reason to distrust them because we trusted them enough to allow each to be around our newborn baby. We raised her to love dogs. She does to this day and has two of her own.

As I thought about it, a scripture came to mind; "Train up a child in the way he should go, and when he is old he will not depart from it." Proverbs 22:6. I realize the scripture is not meant to raise children to love dogs, though that is not a bad thing. It means when our children grow to love God and the things that are about His Kingdom, they will not depart from it.

I can't explain why some young people wander away and never seem to come back to the fold. Maybe the parents did not do a good job in raising them to love God, first. I also have known Godly parents who have agonized and prayed for years for a lost child. Eventually, the child did return. It is like the Prodigal Son who had to come to his senses to realize that home; home with God, is the only place to be.

In today's world, there are many things competing for the attention of our children. As a matter of fact, the world competes for the attention of everyone. As parents and/or mentors, we must pray continually that our children, whether small or grown, will not depart from the ways of God. Our primary responsibility is to live in such a way they will not want to wander.

Maggie with a deflated soccer ball

Percy with my daughter, Molly

Stormy with stuffed toy

Stormy with a chew bone

Stormy and Maggie playing at Smith Mountain Lake

Maggie the day we got her

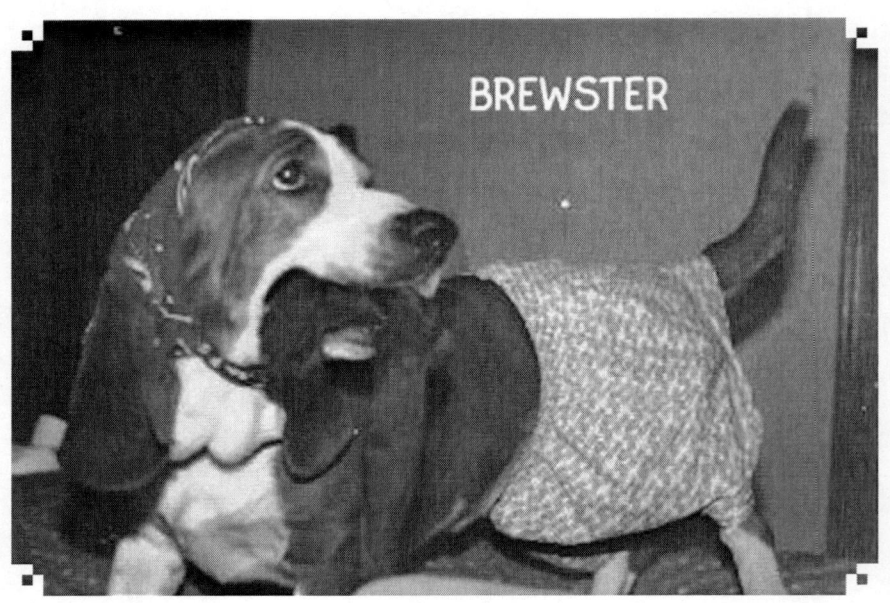

Stormy and Maggie ready to play.

THESE ARE THE DOGS OF MY LIFE

If you have read this book all the way through, you have read about many of the dogs of my life. There are others that did not make the book; Tippy, Buttons, Pee Wee, Specks, Cricket, Nugget, Morgan, Shadrach. I loved them all and I know they loved me. I don't remember much about Tippy or Buttons. I was small when we had them. I have seen photos with each, and it was evident we had a mutual love relationship. I am thankful my parents raised me with pets. I am confident I learned compassion, love, and respect for all living creatures because of the relationship with my dogs. I cannot imagine my life without a dog.

As I think back about all my dogs, I realize each was unique. We owned several different breeds, and many were mixed breeds. It did not matter. They were mine, and I cherished each in spite of their differences. Maybe I even loved them because of their differences.

We live in a diverse world with numerous races, nationalities, ethnicities, backgrounds, life experiences, social order, and economic conditions. I believe I have learned our differences are not as important as those things we have in common.

All people are precious in God's sight. That is the nature of our loving God. The challenge for us is to love as He loves. God does not look at color, nationality, race, or anything else that makes us different. He created us with unique personalities. Perhaps he did that so we might have opportunities to practice patience, love, understanding, tolerance and forgiveness.

I am glad we are different. I am glad my dogs were different. Had they all been the same I would not have learned to look past the superficial but look into what each was created to do; to serve the master in many and diverse ways.

We too must serve our Master wherever we are, no matter what our differences may be with the people with whom we come in contact. Use those opportunities to seek and understand how we may better advance His Kingdom on earth.

In my life, my dogs have been the best teachers about how we are to live and interact with each other. Now, give your canine friend a hug! Then, go into the world and spread the love.

Edwards Brothers Malloy
Thorofare, NJ USA
October 20, 2016